WHAT IF YOU'RE DOING IT RIGHT? FOR TEENS

100 TIPS FOR GETTING THE CONFIDENCE AND HAPPINESS YOU DESERVE

ROBIN BRANDE

RYER PUBLISHING

WHAT IF YOU'RE DOING IT RIGHT?
FOR TEENS
100 Tips for Getting the Confidence and Happiness You Deserve
By Robin Brande

Copyright 2018 by Robin Brande
www.robinbrande.com
Published by Ryer Publishing
www.ryerpublishing.com
Cover art by Natalya Talala and CreativeValuation
Cover design by Ryer Publishing

All rights reserved.

🌼 Created with Vellum

ALSO BY ROBIN BRANDE

Young-Adult

Evolution, Me & Other Freaks of Nature

Fat Cat

Doggirl

Replay

Parallelogram-Series

Into the Parallel

Caught in the Parallel

Seize the Parallel

Beyond the Parallel

Bradamante-Saga

Book of Earth

Book of Water

Dove Season-Series

Dove Season

Finder

Seeker

Believer

Winnie Parsons Mysteries

The Genius Track

A Man of Appetites

A Drop of Sweat

The Long Gray Hook

The Slip of a Rib

Romance

Love Proof

Right On Time

Freefall

Heart of Ice

Fire and Ice

Collections

Mountain Tough

The Love of a Good Dog

Self-Help

What If You're Doing It Right?

What If You're Doing It Right? For Teens

WHAT IF YOU'RE DOING IT RIGHT? FOR TEENS

CONTENTS

1. Making mistakes every single day is NORMAL — 1
2. Go ahead and take up space in the world — 3
3. Be who you intend to be — 4
4. Every day is a fresh chance to begin again. Take it — 6
5. Your ears are the first to hear what you say — 8
6. Be happy with your body now, no exceptions — 10
7. Focus on the right parts of your body — 12
8. Treat your body like a beloved pet — 14
9. Dress for your real life — 16
10. Use your real voice — 18
11. Be your own first friend — 20
12. Talk to yourself like a friend — 22
13. Notice all the things you do right — 24
14. Be willing to be uncommon — 26
15. You're not in trouble — 28
16. You are worth your own time — 30
17. Be willing to admit to your performances — 32
18. Learn to take secret delight in yourself — 34
19. You decide who you are — 36
20. The only way to change is to change — 38
21. Use your imagination to accelerate any change — 40
22. Skip all the extra steps you don't need — 42
23. Keep your destination always on your mind — 44
24. Return to your higher path as soon as possible — 46
25. Live in a way that invites respect — 47
26. Your body is yours alone — 49
27. Fair means fair to you, too — 51
28. Get comfortable saying, "I don't know." — 53

29. Get comfortable saying, "I don't feel that way." — 55
30. Get comfortable being decisive — 57
31. Get comfortable saying, "No." — 59
32. Use the power of "I'll think about it." — 61
33. Enjoy being secretly fierce — 63
34. If you've made a fool of yourself, laugh about it — 65
35. Calm is the ultimate cool — 67
36. Confidence is different from bragging — 69
37. Let others point out your wins — 71
38. Let other people have a word — 73
39. Accept where you are, then go from there — 75
40. Keep your standards high — 77
41. Learn not to worry about what you can't control — 79
42. Know which situations bring out the best in you — 81
43. Watch what other people are doing — 83
44. Build your own internal success file — 85
45. Ask yourself questions — 86
46. Conform yourself to nature — 88
47. Take time to renew yourself every day — 90
48. Create the habit of being happy every day — 92
49. List your loves — 94
50. Live your loves — 96
51. Hug yourself — 98
52. YOU are the special occasion — 100
53. Write to yourself — 102
54. You don't always have to be busy — 104
55. Learn what true freedom is — 106
56. Start living your values and ideals TODAY — 108
57. Treasure your clear mind — 110
58. Honor your fears — 112
59. It's easier to avoid trouble than to get out of it — 114
60. What you feed your mind matters — 116
61. Tell yourself what you most need to hear — 118
62. There is no behind — 120

63. Next time you can make a different choice   122
64. Schedule your day to worry   124
65. Be grateful for how adversity shapes you   126
66. Get up and over your problems   128
67. "That happened. Now what?"   130
68. Stand in the storm   132
69. Give yourself what you've been waiting for   134
70. Choose the people who help you spend your time   136
71. Enjoy the people (and pets) in your life now, today   138
72. Notice what you love about your friends   140
73. Gracefully accept other people's kindness   142
74. Let yourself be the real you   144
75. Accept the truth that not everyone will like you   146
76. Resist the temptation to fix people   148
77. See people for who they are   150
78. Decide if you want to fix a friendship or be free   152
79. Being friends with someone you don't like is a lie   154
80. Be a good friend, but also be good to yourself   156
81. Choose your friends on purpose   158
82. Revenge is a waste of time and energy   160
83. You don't have to raise an army   162
84. Not everyone needs to know what you think   164
85. Obey your instincts   166
86. Look out for yourself and other people   167
87. One and done   169
88. Your dreams want you, too   171
89. Have faith in who you are   173
90. Aim past the target   175
91. If someone can do it, you can do it   177
92. Be willing to be the first at what you want to do   179
93. Suspend your doubt for a time   181
94. It's never the perfect time   183

95. Identify the steps to your dream	185
96. Show others that you take your dream seriously	187
97. Create a career that uniquely matches you	189
98. Being who you are inspires others to do the same	191
99. Be a member of the orchestra	193
100. Your life matters	195
About the Author	197

1

MAKING MISTAKES EVERY SINGLE DAY IS NORMAL

When you were a baby first learning to walk, you fell down a LOT. You probably didn't punch the ground with your little fists and think, "Forget it! I suck at walking! I'll just go back to lying in my crib playing with my toes."

In the same way that younger version of you instinctively embraced the challenge of learning a new skill and growing up in front of his or her own very eyes, you need to give yourself that same permission.

Yes, you will mess up. Yes, sometimes in embarrassing and maybe even serious ways. But you're here to have your own personal experience of living a human life. So live it. Try things. Push yourself. Be smart and kind and do your best, but don't be afraid of not doing everything perfectly.

Yes, you're guaranteed to fall sometimes—so what?

Steady yourself and get back up again. You did it before—lots of times, even before you ever knew how to talk or hold a spoon. You've learned a lot since then. Trust that you're still as brave and capable as you were back when you were small.

2

GO AHEAD AND TAKE UP SPACE IN THE WORLD

You have a right to be here. You were born on this earth and you have a life of your own to live. Embrace that! Be here! Fill out your rightful place in the world.

When you cave in on yourself, slouch, keep your eyes down, try to make yourself seem smaller than you are because that feels safer somehow—you're signaling to your precious self that secretly you believe you're weak. But you're not weak. And you don't have to pretend you are.

So stand up to your full height. Let your chin be level. Look out on the world. Carry yourself as though you already believe right now that you're wonderful and worthy and you're here to live a big life. You're here to be happy. Your body wants to stand tall and carry you like the brave, confident person you are. Let it.

3

BE WHO YOU INTEND TO BE

Do you want to be happy, confident, brave, smart? So do it. Right now. Stop waiting. You don't need anyone's permission to start acting like the person you intend to be.

You're not faking it, you're just skipping the waiting and the steps in between. The truth is, you can change in a moment, like flipping a switch. You decide and you go.

Do you want to be confident? Stand straight, speak with courage in your voice. Look people in the eye when you talk to them. Smile. Think of all the ways a confident person behaves—you've seen actors in movies do it, you've seen people in real life—and don't wait to magically grow into that person some day. It's as simple as stepping into the shower as the old version of yourself, washing her or him away, and then stepping out as the new edition of yourself.

Will people notice? Will your family or friends think

you're strange if you suddenly stop acting shy or insecure or afraid? Maybe, and that's okay. Think to yourself, "This is how I was going to be by the time I was (pick your future age), and I finally realized I didn't have to wait."

The time is now. Go ahead and become the future you.

4

EVERY DAY IS A FRESH CHANCE TO BEGIN AGAIN. TAKE IT

Every night the sun goes down on the day that was. What a wonderful gift.

And every morning you have the opportunity to start fresh. People get excited about New Year's Day because it's so full of new possibilities. But you don't have to wait for New Year's or your birthday or any other special date. Each morning is a reset. Decide how you want to be.

Were you sad yesterday? Angry? Pitiful and hurt? Did you make mistakes and feel foolish or betrayed?

Not today. Today is new. You are new. You decide who you are and how you feel. No one stands between you and the person you prefer to be. Take control of your life. Be in charge of your mood. Your emotions and your behavior belong to you, no one else. You decide.

Let your body help you. Stand up tall. Look into your

own eyes in the mirror. Smile at yourself. Give yourself some words of encouragement: "I love you. You're fun. I like you. You're great." Who wouldn't want to start every day hearing that?

5

YOUR EARS ARE THE FIRST TO HEAR WHAT YOU SAY

So be careful what they hear.

"I'm a terrible driver. I suck at math. I'm ugly. I'm fat. No one likes me. I'm stupid. I never get what I want. Bad stuff always happens to me."

Really? That's what you want to hear coming from your own mouth? Those are really the messages you want coming directly from you in your own voice?

Ask your friends to point out every time you say negative things about yourself. You might be amazed, once you start paying attention. Imagine someone saying those things about your best friend—you'd stick up for her or him, wouldn't you?

Stick up for yourself. Let your ears and your mind hear you saying only kind things about who you are and what you've done. All that kindness adds up quickly to give you a whole new view of yourself.

"I was really nice to myself today."
That's a message worth hearing.

6

BE HAPPY WITH YOUR BODY NOW, NO EXCEPTIONS

You are the whole package: mind, body, and soul.

And in the same way you can't improve your grades or your intelligence by constantly telling yourself you're stupid, you can't help your body find its best health and appearance if you're always at war with it, making sure it knows you're disappointed and angry with how it looks.

So today, begin a new, loving relationship with the physical part of yourself.

Perfection is a myth. And it's a damaging one that keeps us from fully enjoying our lives right now. It's time to fix that.

You can want something different for yourself without hating and condemning where you are. That kind of disappointment in yourself is a poison that keeps you tired and weak and ineffective in boldly moving forward so that you can claim the best for yourself in every area of your life.

So how do you begin to change this? By committing to loving—not just accepting, but *loving*—your wonderful body exactly as it is. You can want the best for it in the future and still love it now in its current wonderful form.

Your love for yourself changes everything. Watch.

7

FOCUS ON THE RIGHT PARTS OF YOUR BODY

Some of us have a hard time liking how we look. But we're focusing on the wrong thing.

Today you will begin a new program of redesigning your relationship with your appearance. If you stick with this and do it every single day, many many times throughout the day, you will notice within a very short time that you've completely changed your feelings.

Start with your eyes and your smile. Every single time you have a moment alone in front of a mirror—whether it's when you're washing your hands or brushing your teeth or just catching sight of yourself as you pass one by—pause and look yourself directly in your own eyes. Notice their beautiful color. Notice the life shining out from behind them. Hold your gaze there and don't look anywhere else. Then smile. A real, genuine, friendly, relaxed, and loving smile.

Then add one more thing: Say out loud to yourself, "Hi! I love you." Smile again. Smile with the warmth and the love that you'd give to a cherished family member or a pet. "I love you! You're wonderful. I mean it!"

This one change in your life can mean more than anything else you ever do.

8

TREAT YOUR BODY LIKE A BELOVED PET

It may seem strange to think of your body as a pet, but it's also the easiest way to understand whether you're being kind to yourself or cruel.

Feed yourself when you're hungry—and make sure you're eating something delicious. Let yourself rest when you're tired. If you're upset or overwhelmed, go somewhere quiet where your mind and your senses can relax. Take yourself out for walks. Breathe the fresh air. You're a physical being, not a robot. Your body needs the good things this earth has to offer.

And for those of you who worry that your bodies are too big, be extra kind to yourself. Wear comfortable clothes. Wear a size that fits. You would never make your dog or cat wear a collar that's too small just to punish it for gaining weight. You wouldn't tell that animal you love, "Don't worry, I know that collar hurts now and you can't breathe, but it's only until you lose the weight. So come on—this should motivate you."

It's a mark of confidence to dress yourself in clothes that fit your body right now, as it is. It shows yourself and the world that you always intend to be treated kindly.

9

DRESS FOR YOUR REAL LIFE

Who are you *really*? What colors and kinds of clothing make you happy? Do you like to wear T-shirts from your favorite movies? Do you like plain clothes that draw very little attention to yourself? Or do you enjoy making a statement with your wardrobe: *Look, here I am!* There is no right or wrong answer. It's all a matter of preference.

But no matter what style and color of clothing you like, make sure that it truly fits *you*—not only your body, but also your particular life.

Think about the activities you do throughout your day. Do you like to get up and go at an instant, take off at a run, rush off to the next exciting thing? Then wear comfortable shoes and comfortable clothing. Make it easy for yourself to move.

Are you more likely to spend hours sitting at a desk or

in front of your computer? Make it easy for your body to sit. Wear comfortable pants that allow your belly to breathe. You're allowed to dress for your real body and your real life.

Other people might wear clothing that looks great on them, but that you know wouldn't look or feel right on you. Be honest with yourself and always dress in a way that matches who you truly are. Then let others look to you as an example: "Oh, you mean I can do that, too?"

10

USE YOUR REAL VOICE

Your real voice is the one you use when someone keeps pestering you to get up. *"All right!"* you finally bellow back. *"I'm awake!"*

That voice comes from your abdomen, not your chest or your throat. It comes from the real you, not the polite or scared or "cute" you.

Your voice and your body are your power. When you talk in a whisper, when you use a small, babyish voice, when you raise the pitch higher than you do when you're talking to your family at home, and when you constantly end your statements as if they're really questions ("That movie was great, right?") you're draining away your natural confidence and power.

You're allowed to have your own opinions. You're allowed to make statements that you know are true. And you can do that in your regular voice without worrying it will come out too strong. Being your real self is strong. And that's exactly what you want.

11

BE YOUR OWN FIRST FRIEND

It's wonderful to have outside friends who cheer us and support us and give us the benefit of all their fun and full personalities. What an enhancement to life! It's why we live among people and not just off in a solitary cave.

But we don't have to depend on other people to fulfill us and give us what we need. That's *our* job.

You are always your own first friend. You have been there with yourself from the very beginning. You know more about your quirks and desires and strengths and weaknesses, more about what you really want and hope and need than anyone else you will ever meet in your life.

And as much as your friends can give you, no one will ever care more about you than you will. This isn't something to be bitter about, it's something to understand and take comfort in. Of course you love yourself. Of course you care how you feel from moment to moment—who else could possibly be as interested in you as you?

What this means is that you never have to worry whether taking care of yourself and doing what you want is selfish. It is selfish, and that's fine. We can still be great friends and family members, while also paying attention to who we really are and what we need. Of course that is our job and no one else's. So confidently step into the role and be the best friend you've ever had.

12

TALK TO YOURSELF LIKE A FRIEND

What is it you need most right now in your life? Is it more love? More kindness? A fresh start? Encouragement? Belief that you can do everything you have in your mind to do?

You don't have to wait any longer for any of those things to come to you from outside. It's time to give them to yourself.

How? With pen and paper. And talking to yourself out loud throughout the day. It's constant, loving attention to who you are, what you dream of doing, what you wonder about and worry about—all of it deserves your time.

So when you wake up in the morning, spend a few moments greeting yourself and asking how you are. How did you sleep? What did you dream about? What do you want to accomplish during the day? What will make you really happy to do or have today? Develop the habit of being your most loving, attentive friend and always taking the time to be interested in what you are thinking and feeling.

Once you're actively involved in your day, still pause whenever you're alone and ask how you're doing. How you're feeling. What you want now. What would make you happy. Then do your best to give all of that to yourself. You never have to wait for someone else to ask or notice who you are or what you need. YOU ask. You give. Now.

13

NOTICE ALL THE THINGS YOU DO RIGHT

It's so easy to keep track of all the mistakes we make all day long. We keep a running catalog in our brains of every embarrassing thing we said, all the foolish things we did, all the many different ways we messed up—

STOP.

Make a new habit. Starting today, keep track of everything you do right. All day long. From the moment you wake up until the moment you fall asleep. Tell yourself so you know you've noticed.

"I love your smile in the mirror."

"Thanks for picking out such comfortable clothes for today—I appreciate that!"

"Wow, that was really nice what you just said to that person."

"Did you see what you just did? You're so smart."

The goal by the end of the day is to get to 90-10: 90%

noticing the good stuff, 10% noticing the bad. You'll be surprised by how easy that is to achieve once you really start paying attention to yourself.

Start now. What good thing do you notice about yourself right now? SAY IT!

14

BE WILLING TO BE UNCOMMON

You are here to lead your own uncommon life. How do you know? Because everything about you is specifically *you*, from the thoughts you have, to the emotions you feel, to all the specific experiences you've had so far in your life. Even your preferences are specifically your own. You might have many things in common with other people, but you know without any doubt that there will only ever be one *you*. This isn't a fanciful idea, it's a scientific, biological fact.

So use that. Be that. Take advantage of that. It might feel safer to try to be like the people you see around you, but what this world really wants and needs is something fresh. Something new and honest and real. Something that comes from the honest, real you and that you're passionate about because it was cooked up in that unique laboratory of your own specific personality and mind.

Being the same is boring. It's a waste. It does nothing to move us forward as a species. And not being yourself does nothing for you, either. You are here to breathe passionate life into the world and your fellow humans by showing us what you think and what you can do. Please give us the best of what you have to give. Go ahead and be uncommon.

15

YOU'RE NOT IN TROUBLE

Memorize this statement: "You're not in trouble for that." It will change your life.

Every single time you catch yourself thinking something critical about what you've done or who you are or how you look, say it out loud: *"You're not in trouble for that."* Think it in your head, too. Repeat it as often as you need to until it finally sinks in. Because it's the truth and you need to know it.

"I was so mean to my mother."

"You're not in trouble for that."

"I failed my test."

"You're not in trouble for that."

"I just ate a whole pint of ice cream."

"Yum. And you're not in trouble for that."

Understanding that you're not in trouble isn't the same

as saying you won't apologize, you won't fix it, you won't do better next time—all of those things are still true.

But believing that you're in trouble on top of it doesn't add anything productive. It only keeps you feeling hopeless and afraid. We ALL make so many mistakes all the time. We're ALL very aware of our imperfections. We keep trying, we keep going, we learn and do better. We want to be good people. And this is how we do it.

Action, always. Moving forward, always. You're not in trouble. Fix what you can and keep going.

16

YOU ARE WORTH YOUR OWN TIME

Are there things you don't do for yourself because you think they'd take too much time?

Things as simple as stopping to shake a pebble out of your shoe instead of putting up with it. Or adjusting some item of clothing that's been chafing you all day. Or stopping what you're doing to go get yourself a drink of water because you're thirsty. Or getting up to use the restroom when you need to instead of continuing to hold it.

You are always worth your own time—*always*. You are worth whatever time you need to keep yourself safe, to make yourself more comfortable, to take care of your physical needs, to rest when you're tired. You are worth the time it takes to make yourself tomato soup and a grilled cheese sandwich if that's what you need right now. You are worth the time it takes to wait for someone to walk you to your car at night—and you're worth your own time to ask.

Taking proper care of yourself is a strong, confident move. You are entitled to your own time—*lots* of it. It's time for you to take it.

17

BE WILLING TO ADMIT TO YOUR PERFORMANCES

We all perform in some way or another, whether it's to other people or even to ourselves. But once we become conscious of those performances, we can start choosing to be our real selves more and more every day.

Are you really shy? Or do you just have a habit of acting shyly in social situations? Those two things are different. Are you afraid of public speaking? Or do you just have the habit of acting like a person who's afraid? You can analyze all of your fears, anxieties, and habitual reactions to situations and ask yourself for each one: Do I really feel this way anymore? Or am I just used to acting like I do?

What if a completely self-confident clone of yourself dropped into your body right now and took over? He or she looks like you, but acts like him- or herself. If that clone took command and started making choices about how to behave in public and act around your friends and how to walk and move and what to do to take care of him- or herself—how different would that new version of you be than the one you've been portraying all this time? What would it be like to do it your confident clone's way for a while, just to see how that feels?

We can always experiment with being other than we are. So try it: Look like yourself but be different. Abandon your habits and performances for a while, and test what is really true. See who you honestly *are*.

18

LEARN TO TAKE SECRET DELIGHT IN YOURSELF

Learn to take secret delight in your own special competence. Are you the most reliable, the calmest in a crisis, the most responsible, most organized, most fun, most … whatever you are, of all your friends? Great. Hold on to that and treasure it in your heart.

You don't need to wait for praise or try to make people understand you're so special—*you* know it, and that's enough. Take your own secret delight in how wonderful you are at something. Your opinion matters as much as everyone else's, and in your opinion, you're superb. Enjoy that. Bask in your own love and praise. Anyone else's compliments are just extra credit. You are your own first audience of everything you do, and *you* can give yourself a standing ovation as often as you like.

"Hey, this was an awesome sandwich you just made for lunch. You're the best cook. Everything you make tastes great." "Wow, I love how witty you just were—you're so much fun." "Did you see how everyone else was freaking out when that happened, and you stayed so calm? I love that about you." On and on, all day long, every single day.

And completely your own delightful secret.

19

YOU DECIDE WHO YOU ARE

On the day you were born you were already yourself. Sometimes it just takes us a while to remember.

And in the meantime, other people are always happy to fill in the gap by telling you who *they* think you are. You're this person's daughter. That person's student. You're the friend who always does X. You're the person who's always been terrible at Y. You're the loud one. The shy one. The list can go on and on.

But finally one day you realize the truth: You can continue allowing other people to tell you who you are and to define your limits and make assumptions about what you're capable of—or you can finally take command and start telling people yourself.

Our own minds are sometimes the one thing holding us back. We've created habits of thinking that make us believe we'll always remain stuck as we are. Or that we'll never achieve what other people can because why should we get to be so great?

Often those habits of thinking are the direct result of listening too long to other people's opinions about yourself. But now you can break free.

Today, listen to *yourself*. Use your real voice and tell yourself who you are, who you can be, and all the things you can achieve. You know the truth. Now live it.

20

THE ONLY WAY TO CHANGE IS TO CHANGE

Change comes to us in one of two ways: either from the outside, through some dramatic or even cataclysmic event, or from the inside, with a decision to change something about our lives on purpose.

Wouldn't you rather be in command of your own life? Wouldn't you rather decide what *you* want instead of letting other people or events shape you in ways you might not intend?

Begin with a very clear picture in your mind of how you want things to be: How you look, how you carry yourself in the world, what ideal work you see yourself doing, what passion projects you pursue, what kinds of relationships you have with friends and loved ones, where you live, how you spend your days—all of it. Take time to really enjoy creating this foundation in your mind. Let your imagination help you fill in as many details as you can. It's even more fun to write all these details down and keep adding and adding more.

Don't worry about how you will accomplish any of this yet. Right now it's as though you're looking at the earth from space: View your whole ideal life on a grand scale, then you can move closer and closer to bring about the details.

For now, remind yourself that the only way to change is to change. Get ready and take joy from that.

21

USE YOUR IMAGINATION TO ACCELERATE ANY CHANGE

Change doesn't have to be hard. It doesn't have to take a long time. You don't need a running start or a gradual series of adjustments. Those "rules" are just habits of thinking. You can change any habit.

What is your image of yourself as a more confident person? See her or him standing and waiting for you, smiling. Then step into that image and take your rightful place. Open your eyes and see through that person's eyes. Let your ears pop open to hear through hers or his. Push your fingers into the edge of that new person's hands, like pushing them into the tips of your gloves.

Then stand up straight. Feel how relaxed this new body is. Feel how it walks and moves. How graceful and assured. Hear how this new confident you uses her or his voice and what that voice says. Maybe its first words are for you: "Hi. I love you. Welcome." If that sounds strange to say out loud, say it in your head. But you will be speaking to yourself often in the coming days, so you might as well begin now.

Do you want to be happier? Step into that happier person. Smile and greet yourself. Do you want to be healthier and fitter? Step into her or him. Begin living as that person does. Go ahead and begin today.

This is simple cause and effect. You and your strong mind and desire are the cause. The effects will catch up soon. Remind yourself often in the beginning: "I am happy. I am fit and strong. I love life and it loves me." Let your desire set the foundation. Change has already begun.

22

SKIP ALL THE EXTRA STEPS YOU DON'T NEED

Sometimes we worry that people will think we're strange if we suddenly start acting in a new way.

Maybe in the past you were used to being angry and pouting for several days if someone made you mad. Now you don't want to do it that way anymore. Or maybe you want to start dressing differently or give up eating meat or make some other obvious change, but you're worried that your friends and family will make it hard for you unless you slow down and let them adjust.

But it's a waste of time to take unnecessary extra steps between where you are now and where you intend to be. Do you want to be happy, successful, confident? How long do you think that should take: a week, two weeks, a month? Would that ease people into getting used to the new you?

If you think a month sounds right, can you shorten it? Would you be comfortable acting differently after three weeks? How about two—can you whittle it down even more?

If you keep thinking about it, you may realize there's no difference between one day and one month: You're still going to change, and this way people can get used to it faster.

Don't wait. Be your best you as soon as possible.

23

KEEP YOUR DESTINATION ALWAYS ON YOUR MIND

Spend time every single day envisioning exactly the life you want, then continue moving every day deliberately in that direction.

Or, if it's easier this way, imagine your best life and your best self a year from now, and then think of all the steps you must have taken to get you there. Reverse-engineer your own happiness and prosperity.

Then imagine yourself five years from now, then ten and so on. What reasonable, identifiable steps did that version of you take to get there? Don't rely on chance or luck or other people doing things for you. What did *you*, the successful you, do right now at the age you are now to get to where you are at that future time?

It's no different from looking at a map and marking where you are now and the distant place you want to go.

There are probably many roads to get to that place. Start moving along just one of them now, today. Then tomorrow look at your map again, make any adjustments you need to to your course, and set off once more with your clear destination in mind.

24

RETURN TO YOUR HIGHER PATH AS SOON AS POSSIBLE

In those times when you know you've stepped off your higher path, immediately stop and get right back on. It only takes a moment from here to there to correct your course. Don't think, "Oh well, I messed up. It's already ruined. I might as well keep going this way."

No. While it's of course best if none of us ever stepped on a wrong road to begin with, that's not how a normal human life usually goes. We all make mistakes. We all fall short. We're living creatures, not robots.

But as soon as you realize you've made a mistake, turn back. Find your right path again. It only takes a thought and a moment.

And next time you'll recognize the danger before you step off your higher path. You'll know what to do to avoid it.

25

LIVE IN A WAY THAT INVITES RESPECT

You don't have to demand respect, just live in a way that invites nothing less.

How we speak about ourselves matters. How we behave in the world matters. We're constantly showing other people whether we value ourselves or not. At the same time, we're teaching them how to treat us.

So if you slump, slouch, keep your eyes on the ground, speak in weak voice, carry yourself as if you believe you're worthless—you're showing people that's how you expect them to treat you.

If you constantly criticize or berate yourself—"I'm so fat/ugly/stupid. I suck at X. I'm the worst at Y"—you're teaching people how to see you. They might have had a higher opinion of you until they heard your own assessment.

Notice how you speak in everyday conversation. If you

constantly begin your sentences with, "This probably doesn't matter, but—" or "This is probably a stupid question, but—" STOP. Think about what you're signaling to other people: *My opinions are worthless. Don't listen to me. Even I don't believe in me.*

Carry yourself with dignity. Speak of yourself with dignity. Treat yourself with kindness and respect. Demonstrate that that's what you expect.

26

YOUR BODY IS YOURS ALONE

You decide who gets to touch your body and how. You decide what feels right and what feels wrong—to *you*. Your own internal reaction is the only test that matters.

So what if someone accuses you of being unfriendly or impolite? You're being friendly and polite to *you*. You matter. Your feelings matter. You have the absolute right and duty to take care of your body and defend its boundaries when someone is making you uncomfortable.

If you had a cat or dog that someone was handling in a way the animal didn't like, you'd speak up. You'd protect your pet. You wouldn't even hesitate. Doesn't the body you've been living with since the day you were born deserve that same love and protection?

Going along with things we don't actually like is just a habit. It's behavior we've learned through repetition. And it can be unlearned in the same way. From now on, pay attention to how you feel around every single person you interact with throughout the day. You might want to hug some of them and run from others.

You decide. You're in command of your own body. No one else is.

27

FAIR MEANS FAIR TO YOU, TOO

It feels so great to be liked. And there's nothing wrong with being an easy-going, agreeable person. Who wouldn't want to hang out with someone like you?

The only problem with that is sometimes you're TOO agreeable. *Too* ready to go along with what everyone else wants, when maybe you want something completely different.

You matter, too. Your life matters. Your feelings matter. And being fair to other people also means being fair to yourself.

So if you've let your friends pick the last five movies and you always go where they want to eat, now is the time to speak up. "Hey, I have an idea, this time let's do X." Fair also means being fair to your friends. They can't read your mind. If you want something different, say so.

Speaking up and being silent are both choices. There is a

right time for both. But you won't know what it feels like to ask for you want you want until you start experiencing that more and more every day.

Today is a great day to start. You have your strong, real voice—use it!

28

GET COMFORTABLE SAYING, "I DON'T KNOW."

Be willing not to know everything. It's so tempting to show that we're smart by having a ready answer to everything, but if you honestly don't know something, be brave and cool enough to say so. It's a mark of confidence. It shows people you're secure enough with yourself to admit that you don't actually know everything there is to know in this world.

We've all seen what the opposite looks like: the person who makes sure everyone knows he or she has already done whatever you're talking about, already knows what you're so excited you just learned—it's so annoying!

If you suspect that even *you* might do that sometimes, it's easy to fix: Be a student of the world. Be a listener. Other people lead such interesting lives. Everyone has a story. You'll be far more enriched and entertained when you're around other people if you let them tell you what they know and what they've done.

And the next time someone—even if it's a teacher or a boss or someone else in authority—asks you a question that you honestly don't know the answer to, say so. "I don't know, but I'd love to find out!"

29

GET COMFORTABLE SAYING, "I DON'T FEEL THAT WAY."

Do you wonder sometimes if your opinions are really your own? We like getting along with people—especially our friends—and so it's natural to like the same things they do and to share the same opinions about people we know and things we see and do.

But do you *really* feel that way? Do you really agree about everything? Or do you just have the habit of going along because you're afraid people will get upset or they won't like you?

You are here to live *your* life. To see the world through *your* eyes. To experience life as you, not as anyone else.

You have your own preferences and feelings. That's normal and natural. Do you ever worry that your fingerprints are different from everyone else's? That your DNA is unique to you? Of course not. This is no different.

You're allowed to think for yourself. What's more, you enrich the people around you when you share with them your own perspective. You're living your real life exactly as yourself—doesn't that sound like the kind of person whose opinions we want to hear?

30

GET COMFORTABLE BEING DECISIVE

Sometimes you might be the only one who will actually take a position.

"What do you want to do tonight?"

"I don't care. What do you want to do?"

"I don't know, whatever."

Life is moving on! Let's make decisions! Even if they're the wrong ones, let's move forward with our lives!

Often it is the fear of making the wrong decision that keeps us from speaking up. But you are here to live life as yourself. With all of your own feelings and preferences. So if you want something, say so. If you don't want something, say that, too.

Strong people boldly make decisions. Confident people say what they think and want.

Becoming stronger and more confident begins with

small actions, one after another, every single day. The more times you practice making decisions, the more comfortable you'll become with it. Don't delay! Start now!

31

GET COMFORTABLE SAYING, "NO."

Just because someone wants something from you, that's not a reason to do it. What *you* want matters. Your wishes and preferences are important. Fair means fair to you, too. So if you're uncomfortable saying no as much as you want, it's time to build that habit so that you feel natural and relaxed every time you say it.

Start by noticing all your easy no's throughout the day: "Do you want cream with that?" "No." "Did you turn in that assignment?" "No." "Did you watch that new video?" "No." Then compare those to the times when you hedge and apologize and add unnecessary words to soften your no so that other people—and to be honest, *you*—might be more comfortable.

But there's no need. No is a fine answer all by itself. It's a strong answer from someone who knows him- or herself and knows what he or she does and doesn't want.

So practice: Say no and don't apologize. Just no. Not no and a cute shrug, just no. Be real. Be strong. You don't have to include a performance with the word.

You can create new habits any time. Saying no simply and without apology becomes easier every time you do it.

32

USE THE POWER OF "I'LL THINK ABOUT IT."

Just because someone wants an answer from you now, that isn't a reason to rush yourself into giving it. Like the Man in Black says in *The Princess Bride* when Inigo Montoya wants to know his true identity: "Get used to disappointment."

Sometimes people are so insistent, we feel pressured to act before we're ready. Or to give them our answer about something before we've thought it through.

Stop. Wait. You are entitled to the time to make decisions. And you are entitled to make those decisions based on what *you* want, not just what the person pressuring you wants. You can take their wishes into consideration, but they aren't the *only* consideration. Fair means fair to you, too.

A woman I know likes to tell people, "If you want my

answer right now, it's no. But if you give me some time to think about it, I might say yes."

People usually back off and give her the time.

And sometimes the answer is still no. Because she's still the one in charge of her own life.

You have just as much power as she does. You know the secret delight of saying no when that's really how you feel. But if you're not completely sure yet whether you want to whip out your *No*, then saying, "I'll think about it" is a strong interim move.

33

ENJOY BEING SECRETLY FIERCE

Have you ever watched a movie where someone starts taunting and eventually attacks a person who seems fragile and weak? But then it turns out the person who was attacked has incredible fighting skills, and he or she swiftly and decisively defeats what seemed like an invincible foe?

You can be that secretly fierce in your own life, whether or not you have impressive physical skills.

Because you have the power of *No*.

There's a feeling of great security in yourself when you know what you will and will not do. What you will and won't allow. What your boundaries are and what treatment and behavior you feel are acceptable, versus what you simply won't tolerate because it violates your values and principles and your sense of what is right in this world.

Some of the nicest people you'll ever meet become

instantly and unapologetically ferocious in the face of injustice, or violence against children or animals, or any number of situations which ignite in them the feeling that they *must* speak out, they *must* act, they *will not* permit this to go on.

You have that same power within you, right now. You can delight in the use of NO whenever someone tries to violate your sense of truth or honor or safety. You are in command of your own life. Use your words to prove it.

34

IF YOU'VE MADE A FOOL OF YOURSELF, LAUGH ABOUT IT

"Ha! I can't believe I just did that!" is so much more confident than getting defensive and angry. It's disarming, too. People won't feel such a need to ridicule or judge you if you're quick to be the first one to laugh at something ridiculous you just did.

But be sure to stop at just that simple statement. You don't need to add, "I'm such a klutz, I'm such an idiot, I'm so stupid," etc. Why? Because your ears hear that, and that's not what you say about yourself. You can admit any mistake without also insulting yourself. Be your own friend.

What if someone else feels the need to insult you? I once witnessed one of the coolest responses from a very confident young woman. Someone made fun of her name, and she answered, "Oh, burn! You got me!" She said it with a big, friendly smile. The other person didn't know what to do. The insulter paused for a moment, then said, "Yeah, but it's actually kind of cool. It's unique."

That's right, Insulters. We're unique.

35

CALM IS THE ULTIMATE COOL

Take pride in being the calmest person you know. Take pride in your lack of drama. If you're not already there, you can teach yourself the habit.

Begin with a decision to always accept everything—everything—for exactly what it is. Then take whatever action you need to in response, without adding the stress of unnecessary emotion.

You drop a glass on the floor and it shatters: That happened. Clean it up. Skip the dramatic, *"Why do bad things always happen to meeee?!"* and just take care of it and move on.

Someone yells at you and tries to create a scene: Don't take the bait. Don't participate. Say, "I understand what you're saying," and walk away. You haven't agreed, you haven't argued, you've simply acknowledged the information. You can decide later in the quiet of your own thoughts whether the person was right or wrong and if you have to deal with the matter further, but in the moment, accept that the person has said that, and move on.

You *can* master your own emotions. Just like you can master your own thoughts. But it begins with the decision that you want to be a calm person. "That's just how I am." And once you've decided, you practice all day long, every day. You will always have plenty of opportunities to exercise your calm. Make it one of your highest priorities.

36

CONFIDENCE IS DIFFERENT FROM BRAGGING

It's wonderful to have a high opinion of yourself—in fact, it's ideal—but self-confidence is very different from bragging. There are things we say in private to ourselves about our fine qualities and accomplishments that aren't appropriate to say in front of others.

Why? Because boasting drives people away. They interpret your behavior in one of two ways: First, that you're secretly insecure and therefore need constant applause and reassurance that you're the best; or second, that you're so confident and self-contained, you don't actually need any friends in your life to make you happy.

Passion, on the other hand, is very different. It invites people in and shows them who you are. "I love playing softball!" "I love playing guitar!" "I love a challenge in math"—those are statements about your passion, not about how great you are at something. "I had so much fun at my dance performance!" is exciting to hear, whether you won an award or not.

Think of the people you're most comfortable being around. Are they relaxed, humble, easy to be with? Or are they always making sure you know they're the best at everything and everyone else is the worst?

Humble is cool. Calm is cool. Passion is the coolest thing of all. Go ahead and tell people what you've done—but share your *love of it,* not how superior you are.

37

LET OTHERS POINT OUT YOUR WINS

Which is more satisfying? Reporting about yourself: "The judges said I was the best they'd ever seen. They all loved me. No one else did as well;" or hearing someone say about you: "You should have seen her! She blew everyone away! She was amazing!"

But what if no one will ever say that about me? you wonder.

Then you continue doing what you're doing.

There's a tradition in martial arts that the higher in rank someone progresses—from white belt to black belt to second-degree black belt and so on—the more humble that person becomes. "The master walks at the side of the road, while the novice swaggers down the center."

The truly confident and powerful person knows her or his own worth without ever needing outside confirmation. She appreciates her many talents and strengths; he values his sharp, clear-thinking mind; she loves herself, heart and soul, for everything she already is. When other people also point out his accomplishments and qualities, he enjoys the praise and recognition, but he still walks humbly at the side of the road with the same confidence and self-assurance he's had all along, even when he was the only one who knew how truly exceptional he was.

Praise will come, but meanwhile you already know who you are. Walk your own path with confidence.

38

LET OTHER PEOPLE HAVE A WORD

"Oh my gosh, she never shuts up!"

A friend of mine once overheard someone saying that about her, and it cut her to the core.

But she also knew it was true.

"I get so nervous," she confided. "I know I babble. But I'm afraid people will get bored. I try to always fill the spaces. I don't ever want there to be dead air."

Of course she's not alone. A lot of us talk more than we need to, especially when we're nervous. Or we say strange, outlandish things that would never come out of our mouths if we were sitting around with family or friends, completely relaxed.

There's something about the public performance aspect of conversation that makes some of us lose our cool.

But there's a cure for that.

It begins with deliberately being the second to speak. It

takes discipline, but you can train yourself to wait for someone else to begin a conversation. And then you train yourself to wait again: this time until the person has completely finished his or her sentence. Talking too much often takes the form of jumping in on other people's sentences because we're so excited about what we're going to say next. STOP. Wait. Be silent. Listen. *Really listen.* Conversation is an art. And you can become a master.

39

ACCEPT WHERE YOU ARE, THEN GO FROM THERE

The strong person—the competent and wise one—recognizes that things are what they are at the moment, and focuses on what she or he can do next. She wastes very little time on regret. She apologizes if she's done something wrong, but then she moves forward, telling herself, *"Next time,* I'll do this instead."

He looks ahead, not behind. He takes action, rather than wallowing and suffering over something that is already in the past and that he can no longer change.

The alternative is an endless whirlpool of going over and over the same scenario in our minds, effectively paralyzing ourselves from doing anything constructive. Practice saying, "It happened. It's true. Move on," as many times as you need to, day after day, until you've developed a new habit of thinking that allows you to deal with facts as they are right now, while you still make a plan for what to do next.

You can have the same attitude toward any of the current circumstances of your life that make you unhappy: Rather than wallow in sadness or self-pity or anger about how things are, accept them. They're true right now. So make a plan. Move forward. Pull yourself out of the whirlpool and take command of your life. Each day is a fresh chance to begin again. Take it.

40

KEEP YOUR STANDARDS HIGH

It's tempting when things aren't exactly going our way to wonder if we're making it too hard for ourselves. Other people seem to succeed at what you're trying, and look: They're not nearly as careful or honest or diligent as you are. So can't you just lower your standards a little?

When I first trained to be a wilderness medic, the instructor always emphasized the importance of doing everything right the first time. When we splinted a broken leg, we should take the time to provide adequate padding around the limb so our bandages wouldn't chafe. We should clean a wound so thoroughly there was no risk of infection, even if it took days to evacuate the person from the mountains.

And any time we bandaged or wrapped an injured body part, we should make sure everything looked properly stabilized and protected, with no flapping loose ends to our cloth or tape. It mattered, he always told us. "We're professionals. We care how our work looks."

Your own high standards show the world who you are. They show what you expect. And they prove that you respect yourself and take yourself seriously. Use my instructor's words to help you stick to your higher path. You *are* a professional at being your true self. How you get where you're going matters.

41

LEARN NOT TO WORRY ABOUT WHAT YOU CAN'T CONTROL

We like to be in charge of everything that affects our lives. We like to feel that we're in command. But the only thing we really have control over is ourselves: our own thoughts and feelings and behaviors.

How can that be enough? How are we supposed to live happy, prosperous lives when we don't know what will happen tomorrow? When anyone can come in and botch up our plans and ruin everything we have?

In the same way you're learning to be calm no matter what happens, you have to let go of trying to predict or control what those events might be.

First, because it creates unnecessary stress—stress that interferes with your clear-thinking mind and makes it harder to know what to do.

Second—and more important—because it's true: You don't control other people and you don't control the world, no matter what a great job you think you could do at that. Accept what's true and continue doing what you can by living to your own high standards.

And know that you *do* have influence over your own immediate circle: friends, family, the people you interact with throughout the day. You affect them with your own attitudes and behaviors. Over time that circle expands outward and you influence more and more people. That's enough. It's what any of us can do. Continue to live as you.

42

KNOW WHICH SITUATIONS BRING OUT THE BEST IN YOU

No one will ever know you as well as you know yourself. And knowing exactly how you react in various situations—for better or for worse—is an important step to self-mastery.

Some people absolutely thrive on competition. It brings out the best in them. They push themselves to try harder, to excel in ways they might not if they continued on their path alone without ever looking around to see what other people are doing.

But for some of us, competition brings out our absolute *worst*. We feel jealous, angry if we don't win, we tense up, we're bitter and unfriendly—there could be a whole host of reactions that show us we don't actually like who we become when we're competing against others.

It's important to examine your feelings and behaviors in a wide variety of situations, and really be honest with yourself about whether you like who you are in those particular moments. And if you don't like that version of yourself, it's within your power to fix it.

How? Either by carefully and deliberately changing your behavior, or by avoiding those situations altogether as much as possible. You might decide that the smartest course is not to participate so you can protect yourself from becoming someone you know you won't like. The wisest people understand themselves.

43

WATCH WHAT OTHER PEOPLE ARE DOING

Look around you. Notice people with the kinds of qualities you want to develop. Is this person happy and at ease with herself? How can you tell? Is it the way she smiles when she talks to people? Is it her ability to laugh at herself when she makes a mistake? Is it how she carries herself as she walks?

Do you admire the way that guy is confident without being arrogant? How does he do it? Is it the way he really listens to people when they talk to him? Is it how he says what he thinks without apologizing for having an opinion? Really notice and identify exactly what you see.

Then, even if you have no aspirations to be a professional actor yourself, you can still use an actor's skill to practice being the kind of person you intend to be. Think about how actors make heroic characters appear heroic. Some of it comes from the lines the screenwriter has written for them to say, but much of it comes from the way the actors hold themselves and move and control their expressions to seem calm while chaos erupts all around them.

When we were little we played make believe all the time. It's still a skill we all have. Use it to your best advantage. Sometimes it's easier to change our behavior and try on a persona before we completely commit our minds. So start acting like the person you intend to be and let the rest of you catch up.

44

BUILD YOUR OWN INTERNAL SUCCESS FILE

Each morning when you wake up, think, "If I get nothing else done today, I want to at least do X"—then make sure you do X as soon as you can.

Whether it's applying for a job or asking a particular person for help, or being nice to someone you felt you were mean to yesterday—take the very first opportunity and DO IT. Every time you succeed at doing something you say you want to do, you build your own internal success file. You're telling yourself—and showing yourself: *Look. When I set my mind to something, I do it. That's just how I am.*

Your positive list of "That's just how I am" can grow daily: "I'm honest. I'm confident. I'm competent. I'm good at figuring stuff out. I'm good at encouraging others. I'm great in a crisis. THAT'S JUST HOW I AM. I'm super organized. I'm the most reliable person I know. That's just how I am."

45

ASK YOURSELF QUESTIONS

Sometimes we feel stuck. Whether it's some mood that we can't seem to pull ourselves out of, or we're indecisive about what to do next in a situation or our lives overall, we can tap into our own innate wisdom if we just take the time to ask ourselves questions out loud.

"What's wrong? Why are you feeling sad?"

"I don't know."

"Well if you did know, what would the answer be?"

"I don't know, I guess it's just because I'm worried about …" And so on.

Or, "I have no idea what I'm supposed to major in in college."

"Well, what do you like?"

"A lot of things, but that doesn't mean I can make a career out of them."

"Tell me all the things you like. Let's make a list."

Holding your conversation out loud, in the privacy of your home or your car, can be the most illuminating ten or fifteen minutes you'll spend in a day. It's even better if you sit down with pen and paper and write out your conversation. Sometimes we don't know what we think until we see it our own handwriting.

You deserve your own attention. You have more answers than you know. Ask.

46

CONFORM YOURSELF TO NATURE

Be natural. You are a biological creature living in a natural environment, and you are allowed to conform to your surroundings. In fact, the more you do, the better you'll feel.

Recognize that there are seasons. Notice that the light is different in winter versus summer. You might have periods of the year when you feel energetic and inspired and you want to accomplish great feats and tackle a whole slew of new projects. Other months you just want to nap.

Your energy levels and enthusiasm can vary throughout the day, too. We can't always control when we have to be alert and perform, but when we're by ourselves we can honor what we need.

So rather than pushing through your fatigue and hunger and pretending they'll go away, how about pausing to take care of yourself instead? The plants and animals in nature don't ignore what they need, they make the effort to get it: more sunlight, more water, whatever food is available at the time. The sun comes up, they wake. The sun goes down, they sleep.

Simple. Natural. Real. Notice your own daily and seasonal rhythms and see how it feels to honor them.

47

TAKE TIME TO RENEW YOURSELF EVERY DAY

You must take time to do nothing. To close your books, put away your phone, lie down or sit quietly in solitude and give your mind its rest. To let all your thoughts stop burbling and churning for a while, until you can imagine your mind is as calm and smooth as the mirrored surface of a lake.

Why, when there's so much to be done?

Because you are a biological system. You are not a machine. For that matter, even metal is known to fatigue and break down over time when it's straining under a constant load.

Which means that you can wait for a crisis to force you to rest, or you can maintain daily command over your own life. Your mind needs renewal. Your body needs rest—not just sleep, but rest while you're still awake. You'll be able to accomplish much more in your active hours if you protect just thirty minutes a day to do nothing.

One way to create a bridge from action to inaction is to ask yourself some questions as you start settling down and making yourself comfortable: "How are you feeling right now? What have you already accomplished today that you're proud of? What else do you want to get done after this rest period? Is there anything you're worried about right now? Tell me." A friendly voice—yours—is the perfect soundtrack to put your mind at ease.

48

CREATE THE HABIT OF BEING HAPPY EVERY DAY

Some people are superstitious about being happy. Or more specifically, about showing it. They think it isn't really possible to be happy every day, and so if things are going well now, it must mean tragedy and disaster are right around the corner. Or they worry that being happy every day is just pretending—no one can really be happy all the time, can they?

Your moods are within your control. It might not feel that way when your mood is dark and you can point to exactly all the reasons why you feel that way. *Things happen*, you might say. *Of course I'm sad/angry/depressed/upset. Anyone would be.*

But you are not just anyone. You are the master of your own mind, your own life, and your own emotions. YOU decide what attitude you want to have as you greet each day. Do you wake up ready for the adventure of your own life? Are you curious what you'll say and do today, how you'll feel? Are you excited to live as *you* for another whole day and watch exactly how *you* do it?

Happiness is a habit. Optimism is a habit. They are choices you can make right now and keep choosing until they truly are your habit. Who do you intend to be? How do you intend to behave and feel? Take command of your life now. Be as spectacular as you were born to be.

49

LIST YOUR LOVES

Do you really know what you love? Not what you're used to saying you love—certain foods, certain books and movies and people, the kind of clothes you typically wear—but what you *really*, honestly love?

What if someone were meeting you for the first time and wanted to know everything about you? "Tell me your favorite movies. What you love to eat. Your favorite books. Your favorite people. Your favorite ways of spending time. Tell me absolutely everything about you! I want to know!"

It's the kind of thing people do when they first fall in love. Which is appropriate, since you can always fall in love with yourself.

So take out a pen and some sheets of notebook paper and start writing. Write fast, don't pause to edit or overthink, just tap into that true part of you who knows exactly who you are and what you love. You might go back to things you loved when you were little, all the way up to something new you discovered yesterday that immediately made you smile.

The real you is here to live life exactly as you—with your specific loves and preferences and joys in this world. Remind yourself what those are. Remind yourself you're *you*.

50

LIVE YOUR LOVES

You are one of a kind. Life is living itself through you. No one will ever live a life with your exact loves and preferences, your exact feelings and talents, your exact thoughts and experiences.

This is wonderful news. And it also creates a certain responsibility to actually notice and enjoy your own life.

Do you love roller coasters and salty snacks and movies about aliens? You should live those loves. Do you prefer being in the fresh air and raising dogs and wearing mismatched socks and watching baseball with your friends? Guess what: Live your loves.

You must always test your preferences to make sure they don't harm anyone else—others deserve their happy lives as well as you do—but that's an easy test. Beyond that, you can just start going down your list of loves every day and giving yourself more of them as often as you can.

You might decide to do laundry because you love the feeling of fresh sheets against your skin. Or you might crumble pretzels on top of your salad. Or call that friend who always makes you feel great. It's your list—live it.

Don't waste the opportunity of being alive on this earth. Life wants to see what you do.

51

HUG YOURSELF

Treat yourself sweetly every day. Find new ways to delight yourself, whether it's baking some food you loved when you were little, or listening to music you love, or shutting the door to your bedroom and dancing and moving in a way that feels great and expressive.

You never have to wait for other people to say kind things to you or to offer you thoughtful little gifts. You are your own first friend. You are in the best position to ask yourself at any moment, "What can I do for you? What would you like? Are you hungry? Are you tired? Do you just need some love and attention? I've got that for you."

One of the best ways to be a friend to yourself is to sit somewhere quiet with a few pages of notebook paper and start having a conversation with yourself on paper. You can always rip it up or shred it later, but sometimes just the act of asking yourself questions and writing down all your thoughts and feelings is better than eating a snack or watching a movie or calling a friend to talk. You are your own friend. Talk to you. Be there for yourself. You are worth your own time and love.

52

YOU ARE THE SPECIAL OCCASION

Are there beautiful items in your life that you never use because you're waiting for a special occasion? Do you have great smelling lotions or bubble bath, beautiful items of clothing, special pretty notebooks, fancy dishes—any material possession that you seem to be perpetually storing for someone else?

You are special enough for all of your things right now. You are the reason to use whatever you own. Part of living a full and wonderful life is appreciating and enjoying everything that has come into your life, whether through gifts or purchases or even wild moments of spending that you end up regretting later, but you still have the stuff.

You are here to experience life as *you*. You are here to explore your own loves and preferences and interests and joys. If you own something beautiful, it's because you wanted that beautiful thing in your life. So why would you keep it stored out of sight and only bring it out for company or friends or holidays? Every day you are your own special company. Every day you are your own friend. Every day is a holiday worth celebrating because *you* are here and living and being the person only you can possibly be.

So smooth on your great-smelling lotion. Use your prettiest dish. Write in your lovely journal. Live now.

53

WRITE TO YOURSELF

Sometimes we don't really know how we feel about something until it comes out of our fingers through a pen onto paper. The physical act of translating your thoughts and feelings into tangible words can often be exactly what you need to understand yourself and your own life.

Although asking yourself questions out loud, as discussed before, is an amazing tool for unraveling some of the issues you face day to day, taking it a step further by actually holding that conversation on paper brings a new and deeper level of self-mastery. Why? Because during the time that you're writing, you are giving yourself your full attention. You're using additional parts of your brain to form sentences on a page. You are more engaged in trying to discover who you are and what you think and how you feel. It's energy completely focused on *you*.

But what if someone finds what you've written? What if someone reads it? If that's something you worry about it, it's going to keep you from being fully honest with yourself. And honesty is what makes the whole process work.

So rip up the pages as soon as you're finished writing. Shred them. You don't have to save them unless you want to. Give yourself that safety and security so you can talk to yourself in private and share with you everything that's on your mind.

54

YOU DON'T ALWAYS HAVE TO BE BUSY

Sometimes we feel guilty if we don't occupy—or at least look like we're occupying—every moment of the day. There's always so much to do: chores, work, studying, the never-ending to-do list. You hate to be caught—even by yourself—just sitting down to take a rest. You should always be doing something, moving on to the next task.

But that's not actually correct. You are a biological system, not a machine. You do not run on batteries or electricity. You are a live creature who responds to the differences in light outside; to the effects of how much sleep you gave yourself the night before; to the quality and quantity of the food and liquids you've put into your body; to the thoughts and emotions occupying your mind. All of those things play a part in how much energy you have, how much enthusiasm you have for the task at hand, how much focus you can give to the particular activity you're about to do.

Have you ever found yourself eating a snack, not because you're hungry, but because at least you're still *doing* something? Or mindlessly clicking from one link to the next on the Internet, because that, too, feels like you're doing something and not just stopping all activity to rest?

A biological system requires rest. That's the only justification you need.

55

LEARN WHAT TRUE FREEDOM IS

Wishing things were different—that you had more power, that you had more money, got better grades, had more friends, were happier, smarter, more successful—wishing for any of those things will never lead to freedom.

Freedom comes from a cold, clear-eyed assessment of where you are and what you're able to do today, under all of your circumstances.

Do you want more freedom at home or work? Prove yourself worthy of others' trust, day after day, consistently. Do you want more people to like you? Start right now being the kind of person others want to be around: happy, enthusiastic, interested in the world and the people you meet. Do you wish you had a romantic partner? Love life, love yourself. Love the creatures you see. Love what you're doing as you do it. A person who lives her or his life with love becomes irresistible. It's not looks that matter most, it's the charisma that comes from being fully and enthusiastically alive.

Each day you have a new opportunity to decide who you will be and what you will do. Our bodies constantly replace old cells with new ones. Who you are now is not who you were a week ago. You are allowed to be new every day. Take command of your life and your choices. Begin again as often as you need to. *That* is your freedom.

56

START LIVING YOUR VALUES AND IDEALS TODAY

It doesn't matter if none of your friends share your view of how to behave, how to eat, what to study, how to treat people, how to dress, what to pursue—are you living their lives, or yours? You don't have to convince anyone that your ideas are the right ones to follow. Just do it. On your own. Don't wait.

You are alive for a reason. Your life and your perspective matter. Your own personal values and ideals shape the decisions you make. Don't worry what others are doing or whether they agree with the choices you feel are right. They answer to themselves. You answer to you.

Open your eyes. See who you are and all the many things you're capable of. Don't wait for permission to be great. You are great. Go be that person this instant. Don't wait to be happy. Choose happiness right now. Leave behind all the negative emotions from your past and simply change directions and head out confidently down a new path.

Expect the best from yourself and your own life. You are here to meet your own high standards. Have the courage to be the quality person you know you are. Let others see your example and choose to do the same.

57

TREASURE YOUR CLEAR MIND

Your strongest, richest asset—the key to your success, your happiness, your wealth, your fame, whatever it is you want—is your own powerful mind. Nothing you can buy or own will ever bring you as much value as the mind you came equipped with on the day you were born and that you've been adding to every second of your life since then. You have a vast store of information, experiences, opinions, and deductions now, and they are yours to protect and preserve.

People who choose to cloud their minds with drugs and alcohol are throwing their treasure in a ditch. They are smearing it with mud and grinding it under their heels. They have no respect for the most valuable asset they'll ever own in their lives.

Let other people devalue their minds if they choose. You can make a different choice.

The easiest method is not to put yourself in situations where other people might pressure you to do what they're doing. But if you find yourself in that situation, have your excuses ready to go: "No, that (drug or drink) gives me a headache." "No, I hate the way that makes me feel." "No, I need to do some clear thinking tomorrow morning." Don't apologize, don't explain any more. Your answer is no, and you are in charge of what you do.

Your mind is your greatest treasure. Protect it.

58

HONOR YOUR FEARS

We all have an animal instinct about what feels safe and what doesn't. The difference between animals and us is that sometimes we try to talk ourselves out of honoring those fears.

True fear isn't the same as being uncomfortable. You might not enjoy public speaking or meeting people for the first time or all sorts of other situations that aren't life-threatening, but still make you very nervous. That's discomfort.

We can learn how to get past challenges like that by practicing being calm in those situations, by taking control of our emotions—there are a lot of strategies for helping us become bolder and braver.

But true fear is something else.

True fear is that sick sensation in your stomach that something isn't right. It's that voice in your head or some internal warning that if you continue staying where you are, something bad is going to happen. You read about people all the time who followed their instinct *not* to go in that building, *not* to get in that car, *not* to go to someone's house, even though they couldn't say why.

Your life is important. Your health and safety are important. If you sense some internal warning that you're in danger, honor that. Immediately. Without apology or embarrassment. Protect your precious self.

59

IT'S EASIER TO AVOID TROUBLE THAN TO GET OUT OF IT

So many times, we know that what we're about to do will bring trouble. We KNOW it, even if we prefer to pretend we don't.

We accept a drink or a drug. We go along with something we know will make us unhappy. We get into the car with someone we feel in our bones isn't safe.

STOP.

In the same way it's dangerous to ever let a criminal take us to a second location—it's much better to fight to get away where you are—it's also smart to avoid taking one more step onto a path you know isn't right.

This applies in day-to-day, less serious situations, too: Whether or not to tell that first lie that will mean you have to keep lying or the whole story will fall apart; whether to give in to someone's demands rather than stand up for yourself at the start, when you know the demands will just keep on coming; whether to buy that package of cookies when you know you'll eat the whole thing in one sitting—so many opportunities all the time not to set even one foot on a road we don't want to walk down.

Exercise your wise judgment. You're in command of your own life. Be alert and turn away from any path you know will bring you trouble. You'll save yourself countless hours of stress and regret. Be honest with yourself and make a better choice.

60

WHAT YOU FEED YOUR MIND MATTERS

Our minds are wonderfully complex processors that can handle abundant amounts of data without much effort on our parts. Information comes in, thoughts go out.

What we might not realize is how much power we can have over our thoughts once we control the kind of data we allow in.

Just as our bodies prosper when we feed them fresh, clean foods and water, our minds maintain their health through a steady diet of uplifting, inspiring, motivating material that spurs us on to do great things with our lives.

Whereas a steady diet of violent images and watching the humiliation of others and feeding off the pain and fear generated by news and even entertainment can leave us upset, hopeless, afraid, despondent, and feeling powerless to do anything of value that might make a change in this world.

What you feed your mind matters. What thoughts you entertain during your many waking hours matters. If you want to live a life of value and purpose, and accomplish great, uncommon things with all of your skills and many talents, then keep your mind free and clean and healthy so that it can think all the great thoughts you will need to lead that uncommon life.

61

TELL YOURSELF WHAT YOU MOST NEED TO HEAR

Decide that from now on you're going to tell yourself "I love you" on as many occasions as you can think of all throughout the day.

When you first wake up: "Hi! Good morning. I love you." When you stand in front of the mirror to get ready: Look into your eyes and give yourself a genuine smile. "I love you! You're wonderful. Have a great day."

When you're waiting in line somewhere or sitting in a crowd or walking to your next destination, say it in your head: "I love you. You're wonderful. I love you."

When you prepare yourself a meal: "That was delicious. Great job. I love you." When you finish a phone call you didn't particularly want to have: "Good job. That was hard. I love you."

When you've made a mistake: "It's okay. You're not in trouble. I love you."

Say it from your heart, say it so it feels natural and easy, say it because it's true.

And finally, when you go to bed: "I love you. Thanks for living another day as you today. I'm proud of you. Good night."

You will heal hurts you didn't even know you have. If you do nothing else in this entire book, do this and you'll change your life.

62

THERE IS NO BEHIND

It's so easy to put pressure on ourselves to meet some particular standard or goal by a certain specific date. And if we miss that deadline, we're failures. We didn't measure up. It's all ruined.

False.

A friend of mine did so poorly in her first year of college, she was put on academic probation. When she met with an advisor to see how she could ever dig herself out of that hole, he suggested she retake one of the classes she failed.

"But then I'll be behind!" she told him.

He looked confused for a moment. "There is no behind," he said. "You're just progressing. This is college. You're doing it."

How many times in your life could you have eased your mind with words just like that? As long as you're still moving forward, trying things, learning, doing your best—aren't you progressing? This is your life, and you're doing it.

The next time you feel like you haven't done something as perfectly as you meant to, or you're disappointed in some result, or you're not where you meant to be by a particular point in time, consider that your next best move is to keep on going. Reset your timeline. Adjust your route. You're doing it. There is no behind.

63

NEXT TIME YOU CAN MAKE A DIFFERENT CHOICE

Don't waste time with regret. Instead, make your next choice.

We all make mistakes. Sometimes horrible ones. But we have to move forward and do better.

This doesn't mean we don't apologize or try to repair any damage if we can, but regret on its own isn't helpful. In fact, it keeps us caught in a whirlpool, just churning around and around and never pulling ourselves out to keep living.

One of the best things you can do for yourself and others after a particularly horrendous mistake is to say, "Next time."

"Next time I'll ask you before I do that."

"Next time I'll be more careful."

"Next time…"

It's not an excuse, it's actually a plan. You mean it.

You've learned why things went wrong, and now you intend to apply that knowledge.

Will it appease people who are angry or upset at what you've done? Maybe not. But for your own life, you have to keep moving forward. The wise person accepts fault, learns from it, and prepares to do things differently next time.

64

SCHEDULE YOUR DAY TO WORRY

One way to practice mastery over your mind and emotions is to choose a specific day and time each week to worry.

And make an agreement with yourself that this is the ONLY time you will worry.

Say you choose Thursdays at 4:00. All week long, anytime something happens that you'd normally and immediately worry about, instead you write down that topic for your Thursday Worry List.

When Thursday at 4:00 arrives, you set aside at least thirty minutes—maybe even an hour, depending on how long the list is—and you go through each item one by one and give it the proper amount of attention.

One of two things will happen:

If it's still something worth worrying about, you will give it your complete focus. Rather than brushing off the problem and telling yourself to get over it, instead you're being the best friend possible to yourself and really hearing everything you have to say.

Or, you'll look at your list and find that many, if not most, of the items aren't problems anymore. Either you've lost interest or they've taken care of themselves. Cross them off the list.

You decide which thoughts get your time and attention. You are in command of your mind.

65

BE GRATEFUL FOR HOW ADVERSITY SHAPES YOU

In the middle of a crisis, the last thing you want to hear is that it's good for you. When you're crying or terrified or enraged or so overwhelmed you can't imagine how it will all turn out right, you have no interest in believing that you might look back on this horrible experience one day and see the value. Or even be grateful for it.

But it's true.

Consider that what feels like a setback is actually a huge push forward. What if you realize later that you never would have changed without it?

And what if that change makes you more of the person you really are, and more of who you always intended to be?

Some people never know how strong and calm and rational and *unbreakable* they actually are until some crisis puts them to the test. They realize they can take it, even when everything seems to go wrong. And maybe it's strange to admit it, but they can even feel secret pride in being that person who held it all together when everyone else had to fall apart.

You need to know who you are—not just on sunny, easy days, but on the stormy ones, too. It's valuable information for you. No one wants hard times—no one. But since hard times do come to all of us at some point or another, why not be the person who becomes that much stronger and better because of it?

66

GET UP AND OVER YOUR PROBLEMS

It's easy to feel overwhelmed and anxious when we're down in the valley in the fog, in the midst of it all. So much is happening, there's so much to do—we can barely catch our breath, let alone think clearly.

Take a few minutes at the start and end of each day to get up and over. Mentally lift yourself up high onto a platform where you can sit with your legs casually swinging over the edge. Then mentally look down on the whole scene below you. What do you see?

What's the larger picture? Where are you in the flow of things that need to be done? How far have you already come? How much have you already accomplished? It's important not to keep driving forward, always doing, without pausing a few times a day to celebrate how far you've already come. Otherwise it's easy to stay overwhelmed, with no end in sight.

Give yourself that time. It might take only five minutes in the morning and another five minutes before bed to do a calm assessment of where you are now and what specific steps you can take next.

Being overwhelmed is a matter of perspective. Lift your view up and over and retake command.

67

"THAT HAPPENED. NOW WHAT?"

Sometimes the best habit we can develop for ourselves is the one the ancient philosopher Epictetus spoke of nearly two thousand years ago: "Learn to wish that everything should come to pass exactly as it does."

Or if not to *wish* it, then at least to accept it as a fact and move on.

When we're in the grip of some crisis we can't believe is happening to us, our minds might still resist the truth. But we can't formulate a plan and act until we understand and believe where we really are.

When you hear stories about people caught up in disasters like plane crashes and earthquakes, fires and floods, there are always those who stay frozen in fear and disbelief, not doing anything to save themselves because their minds haven't caught up with reality yet. If they don't snap out of it quickly, they perish.

Whereas others have taught themselves to recognize the truth when they see it, and to quickly do *something*, even if they're not sure it's right. They can make adjustments as they go. But at least they're moving.

Your thoughts follow their own habits. You can develop a new habit of seeing people and events as they are. You can hope for better and start taking action to get there, but the first step in setting a wise course is to acknowledge *what is right now*.

68

STAND IN THE STORM

There will be troubles in your life. That is just a fact. No human life is without them, and so hoping and pretending otherwise just isn't being honest with yourself.

BUT who you are in the face of your troubles is the key to everything. That is when you find out who you are and how far you have come from the timid, afraid, perhaps even weak version of yourself you once were.

Facing adversity is another time to take secret pride in yourself. *Yes,* you can admit to yourself, *this is a hard time. But look at me. Wow.* Are you calm? Clear-headed? Able to rise to the challenge of dealing with whatever new facts this crisis brings? Are you *proud* of who you are in the moments when everything is *not* wonderful, *not* easy, not at all the way you want things to be? THAT is who the real core you gets to be: strong, resilient, able to put one foot in front of the other and keep going, even as the storm rages all around you.

You have within you everything you need to remain on top of your life. To find a safe haven in your mind while you swing your legs over the edge and gaze down at the troubles below. From this vantage you can use your strong, able mind to see what the next step should be in light of everything that's going on around you. YOU have that power. Delight in it. Use it. Brave, wise *you*.

69

GIVE YOURSELF WHAT YOU'VE BEEN WAITING FOR

You are always your own first friend. That means that you are in the best position to know what you want from moment to moment, whether it's something material and tangible or something invisible like pausing in the midst of turmoil and giving yourself time alone somewhere quiet. Only you know what you need.

It's time to stop waiting for someone else to take care of you.

Everyone is absorbed in his or her own life. People can barely keep up with their own internal demands, let alone monitor and constantly meet yours. If you're resentful that a friend forgot your birthday, or no one seems to notice that you're quieter than usual and more withdrawn, or you wish someone, just once, would offer their support without you having to ask for it—

Stop.

You're stronger than that.

You never have to wait to take care of yourself. You never have to wait to give yourself some kindness you wish someone else would give. Other people's love and attention are extra credit. When they give it, wonderful. When they don't, you still have you.

And you are not the consolation prize. Your own love is the Grand Prize, and you can have it every day, all day long. Give it right now. No waiting required.

70

CHOOSE THE PEOPLE WHO HELP YOU SPEND YOUR TIME

There's a difference between spending your time and wasting it. When people waste your time, you can feel your life dribbling away, moment by moment. All those things you wanted to do for yourself, wanted to experience and accomplish—you feel like you've just lost all that time for no good reason and you can never get it back.

Spending your time, on the other hand, feels wonderful. Because you're exercising your own command over what experiences you want to have and which people you choose to share them with.

You spend your time when you have great conversations with your friends. Or when you pause during the day to write to yourself or give yourself something you need to refresh and cheer you. Or when you stop everything to sit and play with your pet for an hour. Or when you cook a great meal either alone or with someone you love. All of those are deliberate choices about how you want to use your life. No wonder you feel so great afterward.

But some people just want to waste your time with gossiping, complaining, making unfair demands about what you should being doing instead of what you were happily pursuing for yourself—give those people up. Avoid them. Surround yourself with the people who help you spend your time. Your life is your own. Choose for yourself.

71

ENJOY THE PEOPLE (AND PETS) IN YOUR LIFE NOW, TODAY

When you're talking to one of your friends or family members, look them in the eye. Really listen. Be interested. Enjoy who they are and what they add to your life. Enjoy what you feel like when you're fully in the moment with them, giving them your full attention and being 100 percent yourself.

And then if the day comes when they're no longer in your life—whether because your relationship changed, you've gone your separate ways, or maybe the person has died—you can feel happy and grateful for the time you spent together. You know you were fully there, being your honest and wonderful self, listening and laughing and sharing your whole heart and personality. You did your part. You can't control what happens beyond that.

The same is true of the pets in our lives. Do you notice when they walk into your room? Do you smile and greet them by name? Do you reach out to stroke their backs or scratch behind their ears? Do you give them your love and attention throughout the day and show them how glad you are they're in your life?

If so, you're doing your part in that love relationship, too. Then when the day comes—as we know it will—when your beloved pet dies, you can be sad for the loss, but grateful for all the time you had together. Time when you were really, truly *there*.

72

NOTICE WHAT YOU LOVE ABOUT YOUR FRIENDS

We all want to feel valued for the things *we* think are valuable about us. It's the difference between getting a gift anyone might like, and getting a gift you know someone thought about and picked out specifically for *you*.

You want your friends and loved ones to appreciate what it is about you that makes you so likable, so lovable, so special because you're specifically *you*.

Your friends want that, too. It's so easy to just generally like someone, enjoy hanging around with him or her—that's fine. There's nothing wrong with that.

But you can go further. In the same way it's easy to take for granted a beautiful sunset or the delicious taste of something we're used to eating every day, we sometimes forget to pause and notice what it is about our friends that we really love and admire.

Why not take it a step further and actually tell them?

"You're always so calm and level-headed. I really appreciate that about you!" Or "You're so creative. You're so much fun to be around." Anything that lets your friends know that you notice what makes them special.

And then spare a few of those comments for yourself. What makes *you* such a great friend? Tell yourself out loud. "I really love that you make a point of telling your friends why you like them." That's a good place to start!

73

GRACEFULLY ACCEPT OTHER PEOPLE'S KINDNESS

"Oh no, I can't! It's too much! You shouldn't have!"

Yes, you can, and yes, they should.

People like to do nice things—especially if you're a nice person yourself. They might want to give you gifts or pay for the meal or go out of their way to help you when you know it's a great inconvenience.

Let them.

There are usually two things at work when we argue with people over whether we can accept this nice thing they want to do or give: First, we've been taught that's the polite way to behave. We have some inner monitor that says we need to refuse at least two or three times before we finally give in and say thank you—and sometimes say it in a really begrudging way.

It's just a performance. Give it up. It's not real.

The second reason is we don't feel we deserve nice

things. We're worried we don't deserve all this kindness. And so when we turn it away, we're reminding ourselves we have to try harder, we have earn it, and we're not even close to being good enough yet.

Try something different instead: Next time someone does something really nice for you, say, "Thank you so much! That's so wonderful of you. I really appreciate it." It's part of being the new you. And it's what others actually prefer to hear. People like to feel that they're kind.

74

LET YOURSELF BE THE REAL YOU

If you sat down and made a list of all the things you actually like, or even love, and not just the things you pretend to like because your friends do or because other people say they're cool—what would that list look like? How different would it be to start actually doing the things *you* want to do?

Let's say you always go to horror movies with your friends because that's what they like to see. But the truth is, you hate screaming and feeling afraid. What you really want is happy movies about dogs and cats and superheroes. Or animated movies that make you laugh and cry. *That's who you really are.*

There finally comes a time when we have to ask ourselves: If I don't start acting like myself now, then when? When do I finally get to be who I am and say what I want? What, exactly, am I waiting for?

The time will never feel perfect. And you'll never be braver than you are right now. So it's time to act.

The next time your friends say they're going to a gory film, you can have your answer ready in advance: "I think I'll skip this one. I don't really like those. But have a great time—I'll talk to you after!" You don't have to apologize and you don't have to pick a fight—you're just stating your preference like any strong, confident person would.

No one will ever know you better than you do, and it's no one else's job to speak up for you. It's your job. Do it.

75

ACCEPT THE TRUTH THAT NOT EVERYONE WILL LIKE YOU

Assume that at least ten percent—maybe more—of the people you meet or interact with simply won't like you. Test that with your own life: Do you like every single person you meet? Do you make friends with everyone you come across on an average day? Aren't there some people who simply rub you the wrong way, and you don't really understand why? (Or maybe you do, and that's fine, too. Some personality types just never mesh with ours.)

Knowing this is a relief. It means you don't have to work so hard to try to win over absolutely everyone—you can't. That's true. Move on.

Even if you can tell that certain people *might* like you if you just tweaked a few things here and there—how you look, how you act, what you believe, what you say—is that really how you want to run your life? Do you want to mold yourself into what this person or that wants you to be, or would you rather continue being who *you* are, and just search out the people who want *that*? Doesn't that sound easier? And more satisfying in the long run?

If someone really loves mustard, but the only thing a store sells is chocolate, does he or she buy the chocolate and then criticize it for not tasting mustardy enough? Wouldn't a reasonable person leave the store and shop somewhere else? Let the mustard-lovers find their people. You keep being chocolate.

76

RESIST THE TEMPTATION TO FIX PEOPLE

It's so tempting to tell other people what to do. Often it's easier to figure out other people's lives than our own: We can see objectively someone else's mistakes and their best options and the obvious path forward. It's all so clear.

But resist the temptation. Because when you offer someone advice before he or she is ready for it, the person might hear it as criticism, not as help—even though your intentions are good. And then instead of being grateful, he or she becomes defensive or argumentative or hurt. Then it's impossible to hear and take comfort in all your great advice.

It's better to wait until you're asked. Then you can freely offer all of your best suggestions and solutions, and know that they have a better chance of being heard. You've entered into a subtle form of contract: Someone has asked for your help, you're happy to give it, and the other person is ready to receive it.

And what if nothing in particular has happened, but you still have ideas for how someone else can improve his or her life?

Again, keep it to yourself. You are not in charge of the world, just as the world is not in charge of you. Everyone gets to walk his or her own path. Give all your attention to yours.

77

SEE PEOPLE FOR WHO THEY ARE

Does a friend bad-mouth her other friends to you behind their backs? Is someone constantly lying to other people? Pay attention. Notice that. Chances are the lying person is a liar who lies to you, too. That bad-mouthing person is disloyal to all of his or her friends, including you.

The best evidence of who someone is is how he or she acts most of the time. You have an internal animal instinct that warns you when someone isn't safe, isn't right for you, isn't good to be around. Honor that instinct and start withdrawing now. You owe your first duty to take care of yourself.

"But can't people change?" you wonder. Of course. You know from your own personal experience that we can all decide that some behavior no longer serves us, and we can abandon it in a moment. That is the beauty of paying attention to our own lives and personalities and deciding how we want to live.

But change begins with a decision. And you cannot decide for someone else. All you can decide is what *you* will do with the information you have. If your instincts and your experience tell you that you need to keep your distance from someone, honor that. Your safety and your feelings matter.

78

DECIDE IF YOU WANT TO FIX A FRIENDSHIP OR BE FREE

If you keep having problems and conflicts with a friend, ask yourself: Is this really a relationship I want to fix, or do I simply want to be free of it?

Some friendships are forever, and some are just for a season. You like someone a lot, you spend time with him or her, but then something happens and you notice you don't get along with that person as well as you once did or as well as you want.

You have a choice: You can dig to the bottom of the problem, really hash it out, maybe say and hear things that are hurtful but might ultimately help clear the air, or you can decide that no amount of discussion will change the fact that the two of you just don't mesh.

You don't have to pick a fight with someone to end the relationship. You don't have to tell him or her all the reasons why you don't want to be friends anymore. Those words are hurtful. It's what someone will remember. Sometimes it's more of a kindness to simply fade away, while also wishing that person well in your heart.

All people deserve good friends who like them. If that's not you anymore, go.

79

BEING FRIENDS WITH SOMEONE YOU DON'T LIKE IS A LIE

No one wants to hurt someone else's feelings. We imagine how we would feel if a friend suddenly dropped us—we'd be hurt, confused, sad. Or maybe we'd want to confront that person: "Why don't you want to be my friend? What did I do? What's wrong?" And who wants to go through a conversation like that?

So instead we hang on to people we don't honestly like anymore. It might have nothing to do with them: Maybe *we're* the ones who have changed, and so the friendship just isn't a good fit anymore. It's no one's fault, it's just true.

Or maybe that person *has* done something, but you don't want to make an issue out of it and cause a fight. You just want to be free.

If you truly feel that way, don't you think it affects the friendship? If you're suddenly more critical and snappish, less relaxed and happy—don't you think that other person will notice? Why should she be stuck with a friend who doesn't actually like her anymore? How is that fair?

It takes courage to break free, but it's the kind and honest thing to do. And you can minimize the hurt: "I've been going through a lot of changes lately, and I just don't think I'm the right friend for you anymore. But I really want you to be happy and I wish you all the best—I mean it." Be brave and be willing to move on.

80

BE A GOOD FRIEND, BUT ALSO BE GOOD TO YOURSELF

We all want those rock-solid friends who are with us and supporting us no matter what. And it feels good to be that kind of friend ourselves—we can take a lot of pride in that.

But what if your friend is going through something that feels beyond your abilities to heal? Maybe he or she is seriously depressed, or having family or emotional or physical problems that you know are bigger than what the two of you can handle alone.

And to add to the complications, your friend has begged you not to tell anyone else.

There are times in our lives when we have to choose between two very imperfect alternatives. But we must choose. Standing off to the side and hoping matters will magically improve on their own might be a strategy in less serious conditions, but if your friend truly does need help, the right thing to do is to act.

This doesn't mean acting alone.

Even when your friends are hurting, you still owe a responsibility to yourself. And this means you are allowed to ask for help—for yourself. Call an anonymous hotline, talk to a counselor or someone else qualified to give advice. The stress of carrying someone else's burden alone and in secret can quickly overwhelm us. Your first duty is to take care of yourself no matter what.

81

CHOOSE YOUR FRIENDS ON PURPOSE

The people you spend time with affect how you live—for better and for worse.

Sometimes it seems we've gained our friends through default: This one came along with that one, that person was best friends with someone else, and soon you might have a collection of people you wouldn't have chosen for yourself if you'd picked them all from the beginning.

It's good to broaden our range of friendships. Meeting people you might not otherwise have known can be a very fun and enlightening experience.

But it's up to you to decide on a person-by-person basis whether their values match yours. Whether they're respectful and kind to you. Whether you'd want to be friends with each of them independently of the original friend who brought them along.

It's hard sometimes to distance yourself from a group

when you were perfectly happy with it before new people came along. But habit isn't a reason to stay. Nor is nostalgia for the way things were. You get to decide for yourself which friends support and enrich you, and keep the ones who do.

82

REVENGE IS A WASTE OF TIME AND ENERGY

Doing something just to get back at someone is a poor use of time and energy. Put that same energy into doing something nice for yourself. *That's* the kind of payback that feels great: paying yourself back with sweetness and extra love if you feel that someone else has hurt you.

When you plot and scheme and devote your precious mind to trying to make someone else suffer, you steal valuable love and energy from yourself. In effect, you've been hurt twice: once by the person who wronged you, and then again by yourself.

The only people worth your time and attention are the ones who support you and add value to your life. If someone is no longer in that category, celebrate your freedom: He or she was not a true friend. You know the truth now. You can walk away free.

If the person was never a friend, then the separation is even easier. You had nothing invested in believing the two of you shared a connection. If someone has simply chosen you as the target of his or her anger or attack, it isn't your concern once the event has passed. Your concern is always with yourself: What do you need now? How can you help yourself? What can you do to soothe and comfort and protect yourself from any further harm?

Heal your own wounds by loving yourself even more.

83

YOU DON'T HAVE TO RAISE AN ARMY

If someone has done you wrong, you don't need to tell everyone else about it, you don't need to raise an army, you just know if your heart, "That person treated me unfairly (or cruelly or rudely—whatever it is). That is information for me as I decide whether I want to continue to have that person in my life.

"*I* decide who my friends are. Not everyone will like me —I know, because I don't like every single person I meet. I owe it to myself to protect myself from further harm by keeping my distance and waiting to see whether the person truly meant to hurt me, whether he or she apologizes and appears truly sorry. But my days of gossiping, of trying to turn other people against my enemies, are over. I don't ever need to do that. What I choose to do to protect myself from future harm and to treat myself kindly after I've been hurt is enough. I am the only 'army' I need."

Don't you want to know *that* person? He is wise and calm and confident. He takes care of himself. He knows what he does and doesn't want.

That person can be you from this moment on. Holding a grudge, gossiping, endlessly replaying hurts in your mind so you're always keeping them fresh—all of these are habits. You alone decide whether they serve you.

84

NOT EVERYONE NEEDS TO KNOW WHAT YOU THINK

You're allowed to be strategic about your life. In fact, it's a sign of strength and confidence to be in control of what you say, rather than just standing back as words come tumbling out of your mouth. "I couldn't help it!" Yes, you can.

You are the master of what words you choose to use. You are the master of what ideas you decide to share. Before speaking, consider whether what you are about to say will serve you. Does it portray you in the way you want people to see you? Does it reveal more personal information than you truly intend for people to know? Just because you've had a thought, that doesn't mean you have to immediately express it. Sometimes the most powerful and self-assured people are the ones who say the least. Look around you for examples. You'll find that it's true.

Also consider whether what you're about to say will

have the effect you want. If your purpose is to change someone—maybe you don't like how they behave, or how they treat you—then ask yourself whether it's worth your words. If you believe the person will really hear you and change, then go ahead. But you might be better served by keeping your thoughts to yourself and simply walking away.

Strong people, wise people, control what and how much they say. It's a habit anyone can learn.

85

OBEY YOUR INSTINCTS

Be like an animal in nature: Obey your instincts and never feel embarrassed about it.

Do you think a deer in the forest hears a sound and thinks, "Oh, I don't want to hurt that wolf's feelings by running away. I don't want to make it mad. And what if it isn't a wolf, but just a squirrel that snapped a twig? I'll look like an idiot."

No. The deer runs first, cares for itself, and if it's wrong about the danger, fine. It values its own life and always takes action to protect itself.

If a person seems off somehow—impaired or violent or otherwise not safe—leave. Help him or her if you feel the need to by calling someone else to take care of the situation, but love yourself and take care of your precious self first.

You are always your own first line of protection. You deserve your own love and action.

86

LOOK OUT FOR YOURSELF AND OTHER PEOPLE

We human creatures sometimes like the safety of our pack. Even when we're among strangers, we look around and see what other people are doing as a way of deciding what we should do, too.

The problem is that sometimes in a crisis, people still wait to see what others will do. They don't take action. They don't want to look ridiculous and feel like they're overreacting.

Some companies have recognized that human tendency, and they're actually assigned specific employees the job of saying out loud, "Yes, that's the fire alarm going off right now. We need to leave." Because otherwise people wait for someone else to act first.

You can be that first actor. If you notice something—a fire, danger of some sort, someone looking like he or she needs medical help—you can be the person to say something out loud. Or to pull out your phone and call for emergency services. You are a person on this earth, and you have as much right to take action as anyone else.

What you don't need to do—ever—is put yourself in danger. Your first duty is still to protect yourself. This applies especially if you see a crime: Report it from somewhere safe. Otherwise you might become yet another person the rescuers will have to rescue.

87

ONE AND DONE

If someone ever hurts you physically, treats you in a way that's unsafe, violates common rules of friendship or love—go. Recognize that that dog bites. We all make mistakes and misjudge people at times, but once you know that a person is unsafe, it's up to you to be your dearest, most protective and loving friend, and to demand that you never put yourself in danger again.

The person telling you, "I'm sorry," after the fact doesn't cure the problem. Because it's a matter of character. Anyone who would hurt you or treat you in any way that isn't safe is not the right kind of person to have in your life. Apologizing afterward doesn't change what happened. You deserve to be surrounded by people who treasure you as much as you treasure yourself.

But what if the person promises never to do it again?

Again, it's a matter of character. You know in your heart

that there are certain things you could never do to someone else. That is *your* character. Respect it and surround yourself with people who feel the same way.

One single incident of not valuing your safety or welfare is enough. Your duty is to yourself. The wise person walks away from someone unsafe and never puts him- or herself in that danger again.

88

YOUR DREAMS WANT YOU, TOO

If there's a dream in your head, if you're passionate about art or sports or science, believe that that passion is in you for a reason.

What if that path wants you as much as you want it? How would that affect how you live? What would you do, starting today, if you knew in your heart that you were being called to do the thing you love most? How would that affect your choices and behavior?

Some of the best stories begin with some mysterious person appearing in the hero or heroine's life and telling them, "You're special. You have a gift. You have a mission. Let's go." Then it's up to the hero or heroine to decide whether to accept the challenge.

What if someone came into your life today and told you the same thing? Would you be excited? Relieved? Scared?

What if the person who told you that was *you*? What if

some future version of you was calling back to the person you are now and telling you what it already knows: "You're special. You have a gift. You have a mission. Let's go."

Next time you're in front of the mirror, look yourself in the eye and tell yourself those words. Do it twice a day, every day. Your dreams are calling to you for a reason. Be brave and start reaching out to meet them.

89

HAVE FAITH IN WHO YOU ARE

Consider that if you're good at something and you love it, you should do it.

We are born with certain traits: brown or green eyes, large or small feet, a love for music, an affinity toward animals, the ability to run fast, a mathematical mind—whatever it is, it's yours. So many talents and interests in this world, and no one has the exact same combination as you do.

You know that you are unique. You can try to hide it, try to blend in with the crowd, but in your heart you know that you are the only you.

So now what?

Now have faith in who you are. Have faith that who you are is *deliberate*. Trust that your life and your passions and your personality are exactly what they're supposed to be.

Believe that life wants you. Exactly you.

So when you feel drawn to some dream, when simply the thought of it makes you feel so alive you can't imagine spending your precious time here on earth doing anything different, when you pay attention to all of the things you're so good at and that you love to—maybe you already know which path to take. Have courage. Try it.

90

AIM PAST THE TARGET

Imagine you are in a race. You're running hard, pumping your arms, feeling the power in your legs. There's a runner right next to you, racing as hard as you are, but you believe in your heart you can beat him. You know you can win.

Ahead you see the finish line. You can't wait! You drive yourself forward with every ounce of strength you have left, and you've almost reached the finish—

And at the last possible second your opponent surges forward and wins the race. Why?

Because that runner wasn't aiming for the finish line, he was aiming a few feet beyond it. And that kept his momentum going all the way up to and past the line.

It's the same when you're setting goals for yourself and your life. Are they achievable? That's good, but are they *too* achievable? Too easy? Could you push yourself a little past what seems like a comfortable goal, and aim for something bigger?

It's the uncommon people who do uncommon things in this world and with their lives. Would you like that to be you? Be willing to think in larger terms about yourself and what you can do. Aim past the ordinary.

91

IF SOMEONE CAN DO IT, YOU CAN DO IT

Look around you, all over the world, in the media, in business and sports arenas and seats of government and cities and countries everywhere. There are people doing what they imagined doing. No one is born a successful anything—other than a successful baby who made it out of the womb. We all go from there. And you can begin wherever you are, today. This isn't magic—it's not just dreaming—it's being practical and realistic and identifying the steps a person in the position you want to be must have done to get there.

How much did they study? How much did they practice? What did they do to prepare themselves to be great at what they wanted to do?

Be bold. Be willing to tell yourself in very specific terms exactly what kind of person you want to be. Then be scientific about it and write out the obvious steps a person like that most probably takes.

Then? You guessed it: Start doing.

92

BE WILLING TO BE THE FIRST AT WHAT YOU WANT TO DO

One of the best ways to plan out a path to a dream you're passionate about is to find people who are already there and then reverse-engineer their steps. What subjects did they take in school? What part of the country did they move to? What skills did they learn along the way that helped them do what it is you want to do?

But what if there is no one yet? What if despite all your extensive research, it looks like ... it's just you?

FANTASTIC.

You make the rules. You decide what it is about you that makes you perfect for the thing you want to do. You devise your own plan for gathering all the tools and skills and education you want to have to be amazing at what you intend to do.

Look around you in the world at all the people who were first. They are the creators. The makers. The people who used themselves as the template for what kind of person would get to do what they wanted to do.

That's you. You make it. You design it. Then you move.

What's the difference between all the people who said afterward, "Oh, I had that idea too"? They didn't take action. The icons and the visionaries did. The people who were first were willing to be the first. Is that you? Then go.

93

SUSPEND YOUR DOUBT FOR A TIME

In the same way that you can schedule your day to worry, you can decide not to doubt yourself for a specific period of time.

Which is useful when you're about to begin a new project or start pursuing a dream, and you don't want to interfere with your excitement and enthusiasm by doubting that you'll succeed. It's like driving with one foot on the gas pedal and the other on the brake.

So make a deal with yourself: Decide how long you'll allow yourself to have complete faith in what you're about to do. Three months is a good place to start. Mark the date on your calendar and be serious about your agreement: You *will* have a conversation with yourself on that specific day three months from now, and you will express every single one of your fears and doubts about whether you can really succeed.

Maybe by then there will be no argument at all. Maybe your progress will be so clear, you'll be able to make a new deal that day and extend your doubt for another three months. But this isn't a trick: You really will sit down and talk it over with yourself and listen to every fear and concern you have.

A writer I know does this every time she begins writing a new book. She needs to silence any doubts and just do it. Try it yourself. It works.

94

IT'S NEVER THE PERFECT TIME

There are always five more things you can do to get ready. Two more people you need to talk to. Ten more books or articles you need to read before you're really, really sure you know everything you need to know.

Don't wait. Begin anyway.

If the issue is whether you should perform surgery without any training—that's a different matter. But if it's only a question of whether or not to believe in yourself and create a plan of action and start taking steps *today* to become or have what you want—begin.

Theory is wonderful. Dreaming and planning are vital. Having a clear vision of where you want to go helps you direct your course with confidence. But you must finally take *action* or your ship will never leave the shore.

Start pursuing your dream now. Start living like the

person you intend to be now. By tomorrow you'll already be one day better at it. Don't put off for one more day being who you want to be.

95

IDENTIFY THE STEPS TO YOUR DREAM

Who you are and what you want from your life are unique to you. Your dreams and ambitions grow from your own unique personality, mixed with the experiences you've had and the feelings those have created.

But sometimes we worry that what we want is unrealistic. Maybe our family and friends have even told us so. Or maybe it just seems so out of reach and impossible, considering who we are and where we are right now.

It's time to take a step back. Look at your dream from a distance, and analyze it with your logical mind.

Are there other people in the world doing what you want to do? What steps did they take to get there? Don't guess—do research. Use that information to make a specific list of the actions a person can take to end up where you want to go.

And again, if after doing research you find that there is

no one else in the world doing exactly what you want to do, embrace that! You are a pioneer. One day others will look at your life to see how you accomplished what you did.

For now, analyze what skills, education, and experience you might need. Then begin. Today. There are always actions we can take, no matter how small. If your dream is important to you, prove it to yourself by taking whatever first steps you can right away.

96

SHOW OTHERS THAT YOU TAKE YOUR DREAM SERIOUSLY

If you want the people in your life to take your dreams seriously, show them that you already are. Devote your time to the steps you've decided you need to take. Whenever you have a choice of activities, choose to do something —anything—that moves you even one step closer to where you want to go.

Not everyone has an expansive, imaginative mind. Some people truly can't believe in what they don't see. So if your friends or family don't support what you want to do, or seem to take great pleasure in telling you statistics of how few people actually succeed in your intended profession—realize that it's their own lack of imagination rather than a desire to hurt or insult you that drives them to do it. And they might honestly believe they're protecting you from disappointment by helping you be "realistic." That's fine, thank them for the information, no need to argue. But then you can go right back to taking yourself seriously and pursuing all the necessary steps to turn your dream into a reality.

The three main ingredients to achieving your big goals are deciding what you want, believing you can do it, and then going after it with persistence. So decide. Believe. Keep going. And eventually the doubters will see what you've envisioned all along.

97

CREATE A CAREER THAT UNIQUELY MATCHES YOU

One of the questions you may ask when you're talking to yourself out loud or holding a conversation with yourself on paper is what you should do for a career.

This is a great topic to explore on your own before you seek outside advice. You might have better answers than anyone else because you know yourself better than they do.

Start with two lists: First, write down everything you know you're great at—all the skills you've learned and the talents that come naturally to you. Be honest. This isn't a time to be falsely modest or shy.

Second, write down every possible job you've ever heard of that involves the items on your list above. Just list them all—don't edit or restrict them.

Last, start mixing and matching items on that second list to create new possibilities that uniquely fit you—work that you know you're suited for and that you believe you'd be excited to do.

A friend of mine who is about to graduate from college recently did this for herself. She came up with a great idea that combines her natural passion for design with at least ten different ways of using it in a business she can own for herself. And by the way, the degree she's graduating with has nothing to do with any of it.

Your turn. What skills and talents do you want to use to add value to the world? Make your list. Then go.

98

BEING WHO YOU ARE INSPIRES OTHERS TO DO THE SAME

It's exciting to see someone who is real. Don't you love to read an interview with someone famous and find out he or she thinks the same way you do about things and goes through the same doubts and struggles?

And yet still they pursue their passions with persistence because it's what they want to do and they believe they can do it.

It's inspiring. It shows the rest of us what we can do, too. And now is the time to understand and take pleasure from the fact that you, too, will be that inspiration to others.

When you have doubts, when your path isn't as easy as you wanted, when you wonder whether you should keep going or just give up and go back to being ordinary—think of the people following behind. Think of that one person—or perhaps thousands and thousands of people—out there whom you might never meet, who will one day want to retrace how you got to be who you are.

You inspire your friends by being real. You inspire people you come into contact with every day by being kind and thoughtful and also by standing up for yourself and saying what you want. You can't know now what qualities of yours someone else desperately needs to see in action, but trust that whenever you are living as yourself, you are showing the world what can be done. Keep going.

99

BE A MEMBER OF THE ORCHESTRA

To create a full, beautiful-sounding orchestra, some of the musicians have to play violin. Some play clarinets. Some are on drums.

Life is no different. Maybe you have no interest in being a politician. Or a world leader. Or a social worker or psychiatrist. You can admire the people who do those jobs and be grateful that they're in the world, without assuming you need to do that work, too.

We have our own passions and preferences for a reason. We have our own parts to play.

Someone who loves numbers and working in silence might prefer being an accountant instead of a band teacher. Someone who loves reading and writing stories and hates anything having to do with blood should consider being a writer, not a surgeon.

Even your own family members might be perfectly

suited for one line of work, but your own personality and preferences are pushing you in another direction. They're all in the string section, but you know you're an oboe.

You are here to live *your* life as *you*. So be an oboe. Play your heart out. Compose the next great oboe solo that will make us all weep with joy.

The world needs all of its players to come and add their parts. Come and give us yours.

100

YOUR LIFE MATTERS

There's a phrase you need to remember: *A rising tide lifts all boats*. It means that what one person does to improve this world or even his or her small portion of it affects the human race as a whole.

You are part of us. You matter. We need what you can do.

Never doubt that one life, your life, is precious. What you think about is important. What you feel is vital. The person living what he or she considers a small life is as essential to the whole of us as the great politician or the famous humanitarian who seems to be doing such important things in this world.

We all matter. We are all learning. And what we learn, we add to the whole.

What can you do? Even if you have no aspirations to be a famous leader or someone who cures our worst diseases or the person who invents the next great technological breakthrough that will change our world for the better?

Be who you came here to be. Stay awake to your life. Pay attention, don't go back to sleep. Think with your unique mind. Feel your own feelings. Love with all of your heart. Keep living. Keep trying. That's all you ever need to do.

ABOUT THE AUTHOR

Robin Brande is an award-winning author, former trial attorney, black belt in martial arts, Reiki Master, and wilderness medic. Her outdoor adventures range from the Rocky Mountains to the Alps to Iceland.

She writes in multiple genres, including mystery, adventure, fantasy, science fiction, young adult, romance, and self-help.

For more information:
https://robinbrande.com/

For information about new releases, along with special discounts on books and merchandise, subscribe to the Robin Brande newsletter: https://robinbrande.com/pages/subscribe.

www.ingramcontent.com/pod-product-compliance
Lightning Source LLC
Chambersburg PA
CBHW030520080526
44586CB00011B/262